The Summer Anniversaries

THE 1959 LAMONT POETRY SELECTION

THE SUMMER ANNIVERSARIES

by Donald Justice

WESLEYAN UNIVERSITY PRESS
Middletown, Connecticut

Acknowledgments are due to the following publications in whose pages some of these poems originally appeared: *Accent, Furioso, Harper's, Hudson Review, The Nation, New World Writing* (May, 1957), *Paris Review, Poetry, Prairie Schooner, Western Review*. The following poems appeared originally in *The New Yorker*: "Another Song" (originally titled "Tune for a Lonesome Fife"); "Beyond the Hunting Woods"; "Love's Stratagems"; "Song" (originally titled "The Rose-Colored Day"); and the final stanza of "Anniversaries" (originally titled "A Birthday Candle").

Acknowledgments are also due to the Rockefeller Foundation for an Iowa-Rockefeller fellowship during which a number of these poems were written.

ISBN 0-8195-2105-1 (cloth)
ISBN 0-8195-1105-6 (paperback)

Manufactured in the United States of America

First printing February 1960; second printing January 1963; third printing July 1965; fourth printing September 1966. Revised edition 1981.

Library of Congress Cataloging in Publication Data

Justice, Donald Rodney, 1925–
    The summer anniversaries.

    Poems.
    Revision of: 1st ed., 1960.
    "The 1959 Lamont poetry selection"—Half-
title p.
    I. Title.
PS3519.U825S8   1981   811'.54   81-14802
ISBN 0-8195-2105-1   AACR2
ISBN 0-8195-1105-6 (pbk.)

to Jean

O recreate that hour
Divine Mnemosyne,
When all things to the eye
Their early splendors wore.

Contents

Author's Note

Some of the poems from this, my first book, were recently re-vised for a volume of selected poems. A few of those changes I have now had second thoughts about; the rest are incorporated here. In addition, I have felt free to rewrite, in various small ways, whatever else I could, wishing all the while it might be more.

I

Great Leo roared at my birth,
The windowpanes were lit
With stars' applausive light,
And I have heard that the earth
As far away as Japan
Was shaken again and again
The morning I came forth.
Many drew round me then,
Admiring. Beside my bed
The tall aunts prophesied,
And cousins from afar,
Predicting a great career.

At ten there came an hour
When, waking out of ether
Into an autumn weather
Inexpressibly dear,
I was wheeled superb in a chair
Past vacant lots in bloom
With goldenrod and with broom,
In secret proud of the scar
Dividing me from life,
Which I could admire like one
Come down from Mars or the moon,
Standing a little off.

By seventeen I had guessed
That the "really great loneliness"
Of James's governess
Might account for the ghost
On the other side of the lake.
Oh, all that year was lost
Somewhere among the black
Keys of Chopin! I sat
All afternoon after school,
Fingering his ripe heart,
While boys outside in the dirt
Kicked, up and down, their ball.

Thirty today, I saw
The trees flare briefly like
The candles upon a cake
As the sun went down the sky,
A momentary flash,
Yet there was time to wish
Before the light could die,
If I had known what to wish,
As once I must have known,
Bending above the clean,
Candelit tablecloth
To blow them out with a breath.

Song

Morning opened
Like a rose,
And the snow on the roof
Rose-color took.
Oh, how the street
Toward light did leap!
And the lamps went out.
Brightness fell down
From the steeple clock
To the rows of shops
And rippled the bricks
Like the scales of a fish,
And all that day
Was a fairy tale
Told once in a while
To a good child.

To a Ten-Months' Child

for M.M.

Late arrival, no
One would think of blaming you
For hesitating so.

Who, setting his hand to knock
At a door so strange as this one,
Might not draw back?

Certainly, once admitted,
You will be made to feel
Like one of the invited.

Still, because you come
From so remote a kingdom,
You may feel out of place,

Tongue-tied and shy among
So many strangers, all
Babbling a strange tongue.

Well, that's no disgrace.
So might any person
So recently displaced,

Remembering the ocean,
So calm, so lately crossed.

The Poet at Seven

And on the porch, across the upturned chair,
The boy would spread a dingy counterpane
Against the length and majesty of the rain,
And on all fours crawl under it like a bear
To lick his wounds in secret, in his lair;
And afterwards, in the windy yard again,
One hand cocked back, release his paper plane
Frail as a May fly to the faithless air.
And summer evenings he would whirl around
Faster and faster till the drunken ground
Rose up to meet him; sometimes he would squat
Among the low weeds of the vacant lot,
Waiting for dusk and someone dear to come
And whip him down the street, but gently, home.

The Snowfall

The classic landscapes of dreams are not
More pathless, though footprints leading nowhere
Would seem to prove that a people once
Survived for a little even here.

Fragments of a pathetic culture
Remain, the lost mittens of children,
And a single, bright, detasseled snow cap,
Evidence of some frantic migration.

The landmarks are gone. Nevertheless
There is something familiar about this country.
Slowly now we begin to recall

The terrible whispers of our elders
Falling softly about our ears
In childhood, never believed till now.

Landscape with Little Figures

There were some pines, a canal, a piece of sky.
The pines are the houses now of the very poor,
Huddled together, in a blue, ragged wind.
Children go whistling their dogs, down by the mudflats,
Once the canal. There's a red ball lost in the weeds.
It's winter, it's after supper, it's goodbye.
O goodbye to the houses, the children, the little red ball,
And the pieces of sky that will go on falling for days.

On the Death of Friends in Childhood

We shall not ever meet them bearded in heaven,
Nor sunning themselves among the bald of hell;
If anywhere, in the deserted schoolyard at twilight,
Forming a ring, perhaps, or joining hands
In games whose very names we have forgotten.
Come, memory, let us seek them there in the shadows.

Sonnet

for J.B.

The walls surrounding them they never saw;
The angels, often. Angels were as common
As birds or butterflies, but looked more human.
As long as the wings were furled, they felt no awe.
Beasts, too, were friendly. They could find no flaw
In all of Eden: this was the first omen.
The second was the dream which woke the woman.
She dreamed she saw the lion sharpen his claw.
As for the fruit, it had no taste at all.
They had been warned of what was bound to happen.
They had been told of something called the world.
They had been told and told about the wall.
They saw it now; the gate was standing open.
As they advanced, the giant wings unfurled.

A Dream

I woke by first light in a wood
Right in the shadow of a hill
And saw about me in a circle
Many I knew, the dear faces
Of some I recognized as friends.
I knew that I had lost my way.

I asked if any knew the way.
They stared at me like blocks of wood.
They turned their backs on me, those friends,
And struggled up the stubborn hill
Along that road which makes a circle.
No longer could I see their faces.

But there were trees with human faces.
Afraid, I ran a little way
But must have wandered in a circle.
I had not left that human wood;
I was no farther up the hill.
And all the while I heard my friends

Discussing me, but not like friends.
Through gaps in trees I glimpsed their faces.
(The trees grow crooked on that hill.)
Now all at once I saw the way—
Above a clearing in the wood
A lone bird wheeling in a circle,

And in that shadowed space the circle
Of those I thought of still as friends.
I drew near, calling, and the wood
Rang and they turned their deaf faces
This way and that, but not my way.
They rose and stood upon the hill.

And it grew dark. Behind the hill
The sun slid down, a fiery circle;
Screeching, the bird flew on its way.
It was too dark to see my friends.
But then I saw them, and their faces
Were leaning above me like a wood.

Around me they circle on the hill.
But what is wrong with my friends' faces?
Why have they changed that way to wood?

Sestina on Six Words by Weldon Kees

I often wonder about the others
Where they are bound for on the voyage,
What is the reason for their silence,
Was there some reason to go away?
It may be they carry a dark burden,
Expect some harm, or have done harm.

How can we show we mean no harm?
Approach them? But they shy from others.
Offer, perhaps, to share the burden?
They change the subject to the voyage,
Or turn abruptly, slip away,
To brood against the rail in silence.

What is defeated by their silence
More than love, less than harm?
Many already are looking their way,
Pretending not to. Eyes of others
Will follow them now the whole voyage
And add a little to the burden.

Others touch hands to ease the burden,
Or stroll, companionable in silence,
Counting the stars which guide the voyage,
But let the foghorn speak of harm,
Their hearts will stammer like the others',
Their hands seem in each other's way.

It is so obvious, in its way.
Each is alone, each with his burden.
To others always they are others,
And they can never break the silence,
Or touch as strangers but to their harm
Although they make many a voyage.

What can they wish for from the voyage
But to awaken far away
By miracle free from every harm,
Hearing at dawn that sweet burden
The birds cry after a long silence?
Where is that country not like others?

There is no way to ease the burden.
The voyage leads on from harm to harm,
A land of others and of silence.

Here in Katmandu

We have climbed the mountain.
There's nothing more to do.
It is terrible to come down
To the valley
Where, amidst many flowers,
One thinks of snow,

As, formerly, amidst snow,
Climbing the mountain,
One thought of flowers,
Tremulous, ruddy with dew,
In the valley.
One caught their scent coming down.

It is difficult to adjust, once down,
To the absence of snow.
Clear days, from the valley,
One looks up at the mountain.
What else is there to do?
Prayer wheels, flowers!

Let the flowers
Fade, the prayer wheels run down.
What have these to do
With us who have stood atop the snow
Atop the mountain,
Flags seen from the valley?

It might be possible to live in the valley,
To bury oneself among flowers,
If one could forget the mountain,
How, never once looking down,
Stiff, blinded with snow,
One knew what to do.

Meanwhile it is not easy here in Katmandu,
Especially when to the valley
That wind which means snow
Elsewhere, but here means flowers,
Comes down,
As soon it must, from the mountain.

The Metamorphosis

Past Mr. Raven's tavern
Up Cemetery Hill
Around by the Giant Oak
And Drowning Creek gone dry
Into the Hunting Woods
And that was how he went

At his back the wind
Blowing out of heaven
And at his feet foul weeds
That it was like to hell
And scarcely could he draw
Breath and the ribs did ache

No rest got under the oak
Nor water for the wound
Yet kept the way and drew
Home at length to haven
And the familiar hall
His key into the wards

Then owls cried out from the woods
And terrors of that ilk
So that the bitch at heel
A little moaned and whined
As she some fit were having
That back her long legs drew

Whereat his mouth stood dry
And without any words
Despite his heart heaving
And tongue working to speak
Some name to cast the wonder
Straight from his heart whole

Then bent he to the keyhole
Nor might his eyes withdraw
The while the hall unwound
That thing which afterwards
No man should know or its like
Whether dead or living

Southern Gothic

for W.E.B. & P.R.

Something of how the homing bee at dusk
Seems to inquire, perplexed, how there can be
No flowers here, not even withered stalks of flowers,
Conjures a garden where no garden is
And trellises too frail almost to bear
The memory of a rose, much less a rose.
Great oaks, more monumentally great oaks now
Than ever when the living rose was new,
Cast shade that is the more completely shade
Upon a house of broken windows merely
And empty nests up under broken eaves.
No damask any more prevents the moon,
But it unravels, peeling from a wall,
Red roses within roses within roses.

Sonnet to My Father

Father, since always now the death to come
Looks naked out from your eyes into mine,
Almost it seems the death to come is mine
And that I also shall be overcome,
Father, and call for breath when you succumb,
And struggle for your hand as you for mine
In hope of comfort that shall not be mine
Till for the last of me the angel come.
But, father, though with you in part I die
And glimpse beforehand that eternal place
Where we forget the pain that brought us there,
Father, and though you go before me there
And leave this likeness only in your place,
Yet while I live, you do not wholly die.

Beyond the Hunting Woods

I speak of that great house
Beyond the hunting woods,
Turrèted and towered
In nineteenth-century style,
Where fireflies by the hundreds
Leap in the long grass,
Odor of jessamine
And roses, canker-bit,
Recalling famous times
When dame and maiden sipped
Sassafras or wild
Elderberry wine,
While far in the hunting woods
Men after their red hounds
Pursued the mythic beast.

I ask it of a stranger,
In all that great house finding
Not any living thing,
Or of the wind and the weather,
What charm was in that wine
That they should vanish so,
Ladies in their stiff
Bone and clean of limb,
And over the hunting woods

What mist had made them wild
That gentlemen should lose
Not only the beast in view
But Belle and Ginger too,
Nor home from the hunting woods
Ever, ever come?

Tales from a Family Album

How shall I speak of doom, and ours in special,
But as of something altogether common?
No house of Atreus ours, too humble surely,
The family tree a simple chinaberry
Such as springs up in Georgia in a season.
(Under it sags the farmer's broken wagon.)
Nor may I laud it much for shade or beauty,
Yet praise that tree for being prompt to flourish,
Despite the worm and weather out of heaven.

I publish of my folk how they have prospered
With something in the eyes, perhaps inherent,
Or great-winged nose, bespeaking an acquaintance
Not casual and not recent with a monster,
Citing, as an example of some courage,
That aunt, long gone, who kept one in a bird cage
Thirty-odd years in shape of a green parrot,
Nor overcame her fears, yet missed no feeding,
Thrust in the crumbs with thimbles on her fingers.

I had an uncle, long of arm and hairy,
Who seldom spoke in any lady's hearing
Lest that his tongue should light on aught unseemly,
Yet he could treat most kindly with us children
Touching that beast, wholly imaginary,

Which, hunting once, his hounds had got the wind of.
And even of this present generation
There is a cousin of no great removal
On whom the mark is printed of a forepaw.

How shall I speak of doom and not the shadow
Caught in the famished cheeks of those few beauties
My people boast of, being flushed and phthisic?
Of my own childhood I remember dimly
One who died young, though as a hag most toothless,
Her fine hair wintry, from a hard encounter
By moonlight in a dark wood with a stranger,
Who had as well been unicorn or centaur
For all she might recall of him thereafter.

There was a kinsman took up pen and paper
To write our history, at which he perished,
Calling for water and the holy wafer,
Who had, till then, resisted all persuasion.
I pray your mercy on a leaf so shaken,
And mercy likewise on these other fallen,
Torn from the berry-tree in heaven's fashion,
For there was something in their way of going
Put doom upon my tongue and bade me utter.

II

As for the key, we know it must be minor.
B minor, then, as having passed for noble
On one or two occasions. As for the theme,
There being but the one, with variations,
Let it be spoken outright by the oboe
Without apology of any string,
But as a man speaks, openly, his heart
Among old friends, let this be spoken.
                                        Thus.

The major resolution of the minor,
Johann's great signature, would be too noble.
It would do certain violence to our theme.
Therefore see to it that the variations
Keep faith with the plain statement of the oboe.
Entering quietly, let each chastened string
Repeat the lesson she must get by heart,
And without overmuch adornment.
                                        Thus.

Variations on a Theme from James

"large, loose, baggy monsters"

1

It's not a landscape from too near.
Like sorrows, they require some distance
Not to bulk larger than they are.
The risk is, backing off too far.
Once we have found a middle ground,
The warts, the pimples disappear.
There's but a shagginess remains,
An olive or a purple haze,
Which has at least that saving grace
Of average faces, average hills,
A nice, unshaven atmosphere.

2

Whatever goats are climbing there,
Being all invisible,
Animate objects of a will
Contemplative without desire,
Suffer no vertigo at all,
But climb until *our* spirits tire,
Or dine forever, or until

The speculative garbage fail,
Tin cans and comic books, which small,
Imaginary campers there
Forgot against this very hour.

3

Such art has nature in her kind
That in the shaping of a hill
She will take care to leave behind
Some few abutments here and there,
Something to cling to, just in case.
A taste more finical and nice
Would comb out kink and curl alike.
But O ye barbers at your trade,
What more beguiles us? Your coiffures?
Or gold come waterfalling down?

Ladies by Their Windows

1

They lean upon their windows. It is late.
Already it is twilight in the house;
Autumn is in their eyes. Twilit, autumnal—
Thus they regard themselves. What vanities!
As if all nature were a looking glass
To publish the small features of their ruin!

Each evening at their windows they arrive
As if in anticipation of farewells,
Though they would be still lingering if they could,
Weary, yet ever restless for the dance,
Old Cinderellas, hearing midnight strike,
The mouse-drawn coach impatient at the door.

2

The light in going still is golden, still
A single bird is singing in the wood,
Now one, now two, now three, and crickets start,
Bird-song and cricket-sigh; and all the small
Percussion of the grass booms as it can,
And chimes, and tinkles too, *fortissimo*.

It is the lurch and slur the world makes, turning.
It is the sound of turning, of a wheel
Or hand-cranked grinder turning, though more pomp
To this, more fiery particles struck off
At each revolve; and the last turn reveals
The darker side of what was light before.

Six stars shine through the dark, and half a moon!
Night birds go spiralling upwards with a flash
Of silvery underwings, silver ascendings,
The light of stars and of the moon their light,
And water lilies open to the moon,
The moon in wrinkles upon the water's face.

To shine is to be surrounded by the dark,
To glimmer in the very going out,
As stars wink, sinking in the bath of dawn,
Or as a prong of moon prolongs the night—
Superfluous curve!—unused to brilliancies
Which pale her own, yet splurging all she has.

3

So ladies by their windows live and die.
It is a question if they live or die,
As in a stone-wrought frieze of beasts and birds,
The question is, whether they go or stay.

It seems they stay, but rest is motion too,
As these old mimicries of stone imply.

Say, then, they go by staying, bird and beast,
Still gathering momentum out of calm,
Till even stillness seems too much of haste
And haste too still. Say that they live by dying,
These who were warm and beautiful as summer,
Leaning upon their windows looking out,

Summer-surrounded then with leaf and vine,
With alternate sun and shade, these whom the noon
Wound once about with beauty and then unwound,
Whose warmth survives in coldness as of stone,
Beauty in shadows, action in lassitude,
Whose windows are the limits of their lives.

Women in Love

It always comes, and when it comes they know.
To will it is enough to bring them there.
The knack is this, to fasten and not let go.

Their limbs are charmed; they cannot stay or go.
Desire is limbo—they're unhappy there.
It always comes, and when it comes they know.

Their choice of hells would be the one they know.
Dante describes it, the wind circling there.
The knack is this, to fasten and not let go.

The wind carries them where they want to go,
And that seems cruel to strangers passing there.
It always comes, and when it comes they know
The knack is this, to fasten and not let go.

Love's Stratagems

But these maneuverings to avoid
The touching of hands,
These shifts to keep the eyes employed
On objects more or less neutral
(As honor, for the time being, commands)
Will hardly prevent their downfall.

Stronger medicines are needed.
Already they find
None of their stratagems have succeeded,
Nor would have, no,
Not had their eyes been stricken blind,
Hand cut off at the elbow.

A Map of Love

Your face more than others' faces
Maps the half-remembered places
I have come to while I slept—
Continents a dream had kept
Secret from all waking folk
Till to your face I awoke,
And remembered then the shore,
And the dark interior.

Speaking of Islands

You spoke of islands, where the fishing boats
Sleep by the docks like men beside their wives,
Content all night, while under them the waves,
Arching their backs a little, purr like cats
And rub against them peacefully. Some nights,
You said, nothing in all that harbor moves
Except those boats with motion of those waves
And a few sleepy gulls with cries like flutes.

You spoke of islands as I speak of you,
Sea-circled and remote, an island too,
And of such latitudes as islands keep,
And langorous airs, and fragrances offshore,
And blue approaches to desire and sleep,
O my belle harbor, my San Salvador!

Sonnet about P.

A woman I knew had seemed most beautiful
For being cold and difficult of access.
I saw my friend, the cleverest man of us,
But for a word from her to make him whole,
Himself fall speechless, like a boy at school,
And others also, followers of the chase,
Look up or down but not into that face,
Owing to the perfection of the skull.
I knew this lady a dozen years ago.
Since, that she has to two or three been kind,
After long siege, and these not of her sort,
And that she has both given and taken hurt,
Hearing all this, and more, I call to mind
That high, improbable bosom, which was snow.

Another Song

Merry the green, the green hill shall be merry.
Hungry, the owlet shall seek out the mouse,
And Jack his Joan, but they shall never marry.

And snows shall fly, the big flakes fat and furry.
Lonely, the traveler shall seek out the house,
And Jack his Joan, but they shall never marry.

Weary the soldiers go, and come back weary,
Up a green hill and down the withered hill,
And Jack from Joan, and they shall never marry.

In Bertram's Garden

Jane looks down at her organdy skirt
As if *it* somehow were the thing disgraced,
For being there, on the floor, in the dirt,
And she catches it up about her waist,
Smooths it out along one hip,
And pulls it over the crumpled slip.

On the porch, green-shuttered, cool,
Asleep is Bertram, that bronze boy,
Who, having wound her around a spool,
Sends her spinning like a toy
Out to the garden, all alone,
To sit and weep on a bench of stone.

Soon the purple dark will bruise
Lily and bleeding heart and rose,
And the little Cupid lose
Eyes and ears and chin and nose,
And Jane lie down with others soon
Naked to the naked moon.

The Stray Dog by the Summerhouse

This morning, down
By the summerhouse,
I saw a stray,
A stray dog dead.
All white and brown
The dead friend lay,
All brown with a white
Mark on his head.
His eyes were bright
And open wide,
Bright, open eyes
With worms inside,
And the tongue hung loose
To the butterflies,
The butterflies
And the flying ants.

And because of the tongue
He seemed like one
Who has run too long,
And stops, and pants.
And because of the sun
There came a scent,
And it was strong.
It came and went

As if somewhere near
A round, ripe pear,
So ripe, so round,
Had dropped to the ground
And with the heat
Was turning black.
And the scent came back,
And it was sweet.

Anthony St. Blues

1

Morning. The roofs emerge, the yard—
Brown grass, puddled with snow, dog's bone—
Emerges, but not yet comes forth
Her plumber from the widow's arms,
To touch his dreaming truck awake
That all night slumbered by the curb,
Nor yet the lame child from his race,
His dog from rat and squirrel. Only,
At the horizon, pines release
Starlings to blacken wires with day.

2

Evening. The paper-boy on wheels
Turns at his corner into night.
The one-armed man, returning late,
Stoops to retrieve the murderous news,
Tucks it beneath the willing stump,
And mounts once more with slippery care
The purgatory of the stoop.
Withindoors many now enact,
Behind drawn shades, their shadow lives.
The headlights, turning, grope their way.

A Winter Ode to the Old Men of Lummus Park, Miami, Florida

Risen from rented rooms, old ghosts
Come back to haunt our parks by day,
They creep up Fifth Street through the crowd,
Unseeing and almost unseen,
Halting before the shops for breath,
Still proud, pretending to admire
The fat hens dressed and hung for flies
There, or perhaps the lone, dead fern
Dressing the window of a small
Hotel. Winter has blown them south—
How many? Twelve in Lummus Park
I count now, shivering where they stand,
A little thicket of thin trees,
And more on benches turning with
The sun, wan heliotropes, all day.

O you who wear against the breast
The torturous flannel undervest
Winter and summer, yet are cold,
Poor cracked thermometers stuck now
At zero everlastingly,
Old men, bent like your walking sticks
As with the pressure of some hand,
Surely we must have thought you strong
To lean on you so hard, so long!

Counting the Mad

This one was put in a jacket,
This one was sent home,
This one was given bread and meat
But would eat none,
And this one cried No No No No
All day long.

This one looked at the window
As though it were a wall,
This one saw things that were not there,
This one things that were,
And this one cried No No No No
All day long.

This one thought himself a bird,
This one a dog,
And this one thought himself a man,
An ordinary man,
And cried and cried No No No No
All day long.

On a Painting by Patient B of the Independence State Hospital for the Insane

Who named the clouds Rabbit, Bear, and Hyena

1

These seven houses have learned to face one another,
But not at the expected angles. Those silly brown lumps,
That are probably meant for hills and not other houses,
After ages of being themselves, though naturally slow,
Are learning to be exclusive without offending.
The arches and entrances (down to the right out of sight)
Have mastered the lesson of remaining closed.
And even the skies keep a certain understandable distance,
For these are the houses of the very rich.

2

One sees their children playing with leopards, tamed
At great cost, or perhaps it is only other children,
For none of these objects is anything more than a spot,
And perhaps there are not any children but only leopards
Playing with leopards, and perhaps there are only the spots.
And the little maids that hang from the windows like
    tongues,
Calling the children in, admiring the leopards,

Are the dashes a child might represent motion by means of,
Or dazzlement possibly, the brillance of solid-gold houses.

3

The clouds resemble those empty balloons in cartoons
Which approximate silence. These clouds, if clouds they
     are
(And not the smoke from the seven aspiring chimneys),
The more one studies them the more it appears
They too have expressions. One might almost say
They have their habits, their wrong opinions, that their
Impassivity masks an essentially lovable foolishness,
And they will be given names by those who live under
     them
Not public like mountains' but private like companions'.

To Satan in Heaven

Forgive, Satan, virtue's pedants, all those
Who have broken their habits, or had none,
The keepers of promises, prize-winners,
Meek as leaves in the wind's circus, evenings;
And these forgive who have forgotten how,
The melancholy, who, lacing a shoe,
Choose not to continue, the merely bored,
Who have modeled their lives after cloud-shapes;
For which confessing, have mercy on them,
The different and the indifferent,
In inverse proportion to their merit,
As upon us also, who have seen thee
Shyly in mirrors by morning, shaving,
Or head in loose curls on the next pillow,
Reduced thus to our own scope and purpose,
Satan, who, though in heaven, downward yearned,
As the butterfly, weary of flowers,
Longs for the cocoon or the looping net.

About the Author

Donald Justice is professor of English at the University of Iowa, and earlier taught at Syracuse University, the University of California, Irvine, Princeton University and the University of Virginia. *The Summer* Anniversaries is his first collection of poems, *Night Light*, also published by Wesleyan, his second. He won the Pulitzer Prize for Poetry in 1980 for his *Selected Poems*. His home is in Iowa City.